I dedicate this book to all of you who have dreams but have been short on the courage to pursue them. If this book can provide you with the needed encouragement, then for me, it will have been worth the writing.

10 Birds with 1 Stone

POLLINATOR PRESS

560 Second Street
Oakland, CA 94607

www.pollinatorpress.com

This book is available for special promotions and premiums. For details contact Pollinator Press.

First Edition 2006
Printed in the United States of America
10 9 8 7 6 5 4 3 2 1
ISBN 0-9774410-0-8

10 BIRDS WITH 1 STONE

MERRITT SHER

AUTHOR'S NOTE

Over the years, I've enjoyed summing up a meeting or distilling a collection of ideas by writing a kind of philosophical snippet. These sometime give clarity to complex issues and people frequently write them down for later use. I've coined hundreds of them by now, but for this book I've selected fifty-two for your consideration.

I believe they have broad applications for finding success in business and in life, but the details I leave to be filled in by you.

ACKNOWLEDGEMENTS

Some time ago it was suggested to me that I put my collection of musings into a book. As it seemed like a good idea, I enlisted the help of Susan Mills, who worked in the Terranomics marketing department. I thank Susan for helping me begin the process. Margaret Partlow, my assistant for the past ten years, worked with me to further organize the material. With her excellent help we made good progress. I thank Margaret for the focus and support she provided then, and continues to provide. I thank Mark Seiler and Lynne Bremer for their vital input. David Latimer, a publisher and friend who is familiar with my aphoristic tendencies helped me select the top 52. David brought Wendy Braitman as a consultant, Sylvia Thyssen as proofreader and Ryder Carroll for book design and illustrations. Thank you David, and your team, for completing the project with me. I thank my wife Pam and my three kids for their unflagging support and finally my sister Abby who made sure it hung together.

TABLE OF CONTENTS

10 BIRDS WITH 1 STONE

BELIEVING CREATES POTENTIAL

If you can visualize an idea, you can make it happen. Wait for the moment when you see the vision clearly. Once you do, that image will always be there. When you visualize an idea, you are actually seeing an end result which you can then reference. Is what you are doing now going to allow your vision to unfold? How do you continue moving forward bringing in people, substantive elements, and the infrastructure needed to achieve the potential? It all begins with belief. Challenge yourself to trust in your intuition and beliefs. When you visualize something, a pattern begins to evolve around the vision. If your idea is properly aligned, the pattern will move in the right direction on its own.

CREATIVE DESTRUCTION

The defining quality of entrepreneurship is creative destruction. As an entrepreneur you are destroying an existing form and making something new out of it. Being an entrepreneur means proactively changing the system as opposed to just connecting the pieces or putting the pieces in play. It's grabbing a construct, tearing it apart, and putting it back together again in a different way. By destroying an existing form, you release the energy necessary to create something new.

THE AUTHENTIC CORE

The stronger core concept you have, the better suited you are for success. Once you've determined the concept, ask yourself if your actions are adding to or subtracting from the core. When you present a cohesive and consistent message, people will feel it, identify with it, and become attracted to it. When starting a project or building an organization, make certain that every element adds to the strength and solidarity of what you are doing.

THE BIG PICTURE

Strive to see the issues clearly. What are the long-term objectives? Envision the possibilities in all the factors that influence your world. Does the complete picture look right? Imagine the largest application of your ideas and the grandest vision of your success. Intermediate obstacles will dim by the force of the larger vision.

BUILD THE MAGNET
START THE PROCESS

Build your idea as if it were a magnet. Gather sufficient information and involve enough people in your vision that personalities and motivations can react and catalyze ideas into action. The magnetic process will attract more people and resources, creating an even bigger, stronger magnet. You will be creating a buzz or a bandwagon effect. When you've built the magnet correctly, people will be drawn to your ideas. Identify the raw ingredients in your surroundings, resources, and connections so they can be utilized to attract others.

YOU CAN ONLY BE SO ORIGINAL
WITH THE ORDINARY

GETTING PAST THE REALITY BLOCK

Do things in an unlikely way. When proposing an innovative idea, be prepared to encounter stiff resistance from peers, lending organizations, and the public at large. Good ideas are often a little off base. If your vision is really original, you stand the chance of being considered a kook. But an amazing thing happens when you are successful in implementing an original idea. Suddenly you are considered a visionary. Proving that your vision is right will lend credibility to more of your ideas.

HANG A SITE PLAN ON THE WALL

When you first envision a project, you need to find a place to start. A concept loosely understood requires a form that will allow you to test its validity. Hanging a site plan on the wall will help you build real objects from abstract ideas. Put up a number of versions and test your assumptions. This will usually result in changes. The site plan, incorporated into your daily awareness, will act as a filter to provide you with the necessary information to make corrections. After you have been through this process a number of times, you may get to a point where you have included every element in its best possible form. Then you can proceed to the next level.

IF MORE THAN 25% WORKS,
IT'S NOT CREATIVE ENOUGH

When you're thinking of starting a new venture, you will generate a lot of ideas, many of which will be shot down. This will give you the opportunity to learn and move forward. Many ideas won't stand up in the marketplace or stand up to implementation. In order to build a firm foundation, you need to fully explore the environment. Ideas are always in the process of formation. Don't be discouraged by a high rate of failure or negative comments by friends, family and associates. If you assume you'll succeed all of the time, you're expecting too much.

FIND INSPIRATION, BUT DON'T COPY

AT THE LAST MOMENT
THE BEST DEAL POPS UP

Don't commit too early. By developing an enthusiastic base for your idea, you can create a feeding frenzy. After one person perceives value, other people will follow. You then have a chance to draw from a wider range of choices. This process becomes exponential. Make deals that allow for maximum flexibility. Realize that the last moment has the most potential for the best ingredients to pop up.

TEN BIRDS WITH ONE STONE

Design your actions to have a multiplicity of impacts. This approach is a great source of power. In bowling, when you hit the king pin, all the other pins work together to create a strike. Potential. Sequential. The entrepreneur who understands all the implications of an action is the most powerful. People are often able to see just one or two moves ahead. The implications of any action are much more complex and multifold. Train yourself to see disparate connections, to anticipate the unlikely outcome, and to synthesize the results of multiple moves. While working within a frame of reference, always keep your antennae out there.

TRY ON THE CONCEPT
LEARN WHAT'S RIGHT
LEARN WHAT'S WRONG

When you undertake something new, get feedback before you make major decisions. Ask all kinds of people what they think. Get opinions from experts and people you value as well as from those who know little about your endeavor. A broad range of sources will give you diverse information, and you will achieve a better result.

ALLOW THINGS TO BE
AS THEY WANT TO BE

The natural order is the best order. The public will continue to be drawn to places, systems and ideas that feel comfortable and natural. When you are creating something new, you may not get the result you originally sought because the natural result is different from your plan. Execute your plan, but allow things to unfold as they want to be. If it feels good, shape and encourage the direction. You will get something much better than you first intended.

IF IT DOESN'T FEEL
RIGHT IT ISN'T

BUILD PLATFORMS

Think of a platform as a way station or an intermediate goal. It is similar to resting at base camp and planning your ascent to the mountain summit. A chance to re-energize and chart your next move. Any mission, campaign, or objective needs intermediate goals. When you undertake a long journey, know how many steps there are between resting places.

PRESENT RADICAL IDEAS IN A NON-THREATENING MANNER

Understand how people respond to new ideas. If you shock or confuse people, they will likely reject the idea. When presenting new concepts that might be viewed as extreme, do so in a way that will not be threatening. Occasionally an idea is so essential and compelling that it is quickly understood despite being presented in a radical way. This is not always the case. Often, good ideas are rejected because the timing and presentation are wrong. Anticipating this will keep you from being discouraged. If your idea is rejected, seek more input and remain flexible. Your idea will find its place if it is not abandoned. Many concepts you develop may have to be put on the shelf temporarily as part of a broader strategy, but they will emerge at the appropriate time.

BE INVOLVED, THEY EVOLVE

Commit yourself to the project. Your involvement fertilizes the terrain, energizes other elements, and provides a ground for others to build on. Your vision, once articulated, will gain momentum, evolve, and grow. The next step is to incorporate people into the process. Open the door to your vision so that others can see new possibilities. Show the way by your commitment and enthusiasm, and others will feel empowered to take on challenges and grow the project.

DO PEOPLE ADD OR DETRACT ?

Avoid people who draw energy away from you. Find people with positive energy to enhance your vision and you will be more creative and successful. People who are not suited for the corporate world are often the most creative, and they can add the most to your project even though their creativity often goes unrecognized by society at large. Look for venues that attract creative people who will identify with your core values. The right staff will make for favorable dynamics in the workplace. A workforce will have many identities coming into play. Listen for the right wavelength in people, and recognize those with excitement for the project, a personal affinity with you, and a dynamic energy and attitude.

WHEN ONE THING CHANGES, EVERYTHING CHANGES

STIRRING AND SORTING

Expose your mind to new ideas. Disrupt the status quo. Make an effort to meet new people. Put yourself in new and novel situations. Questioning basic assumptions is an example of "stirring." Assessing new information, categorizing contacts and cataloging experience arc cxamples of "sorting." Periodically, it helps to stir and sort. Keep it fresh and reorder it. If things are stagnant, you must introduce new elements. By sorting through the relevant ideas of the moment you point yourself in a new direction.

MAKING SOMEWHERE
OUT OF NOWHERE

Every place has the potential to become greater than its current form suggests. Identify and promote the unique characteristics of a place and challenge the thought dynamics that limit and define it. Highlight the location's strategic importance or create a renewed vision of its identity. Package the best natural attributes rather than creating an artificial identity. Characteristics that can be affected with the least amount of effort should be tackled first. Artistic people are among the first to recognize the possibilities in places, so cultivate the more artistic elements and the mainstream will follow.

WHEN THE IDEA GETS OUT
IT GROWS TO CONSENSUS

If you want an idea to get into the market-place, present it with authority. An initial group will respond to a good idea and begin adopting it, and eventually the acceptance will become more widespread. Your ideas face competition with other ideas and may be met with indifference or rejection. But what is at first considered outrageous slowly becomes acceptable, then desirable, and finally essential. Effective marketing, public relations, endorsements, and word of mouth can artificially accelerate the process of consensus building; but if forced, they can pollute the idea. Intangible elements, unpredictable events, or even lucky timing can lend tremendous power and momentum toward the acceptance of an idea.

IT'S HARD TO RECOGNIZE
EXCELLENCE WHEN IT COMES
IN AN UNRECOGNIZABLE FORM

Often people try to analogize new ideas comparing them with something familiar. If they have never been exposed to a concept that's been put together in an unusual way, they often think it won't work. If a new concept holds no recognizable form, people are unlikely to embrace it. It's your job to provide a frame of reference so others can understand the validity and value of the idea. Keep reinforcing your idea. The faint-hearted need more reinforcement.

INCREMENTAL CHANGES
OR DRAMATIC MOVES

Should you change incrementally or dramatically? Both approaches will work, depending on the situation. Don't commit to one strategy over the other. Be flexible. Making incremental changes can keep up momentum, and momentum often results in greater opportunity. But there is also a time to abandon an evolutionary approach in favor of a dramatic move. Learn to assess the best way to act.

PURSUE PARALLEL TRACKS

Work on at least two ideas or strategies simultaneously. This helps to insure that you're left with an alternative if your primary strategy doesn't work out. It also gives you the option of toggling between one strategy and another. If both strategies work, you will have more flexibility and a greater ability to move forward with a better result. More options equal more control.

KEEP ON THE TRAIL WHILE IT'S HOT
TAKE A BREAK WHEN IT'S NOT

THE FUNK OF BEING STUCK - HOW LONG CAN YOU WAIT?

We all get stuck sometimes, and we tend to get into a funk when it happens. Feel the funk! It's okay to stay in it for awhile. Your pathway may be blocked with old ideas or unfulfilled expectations and disappointments. Clear the old ideas away first. Think about new and extreme avenues. Then be patient. The energy needed to get out of the funk takes awhile to gestate. If you pay attention, you will naturally know when to move on.

THE UNEXPECTED REINFORCEMENT

deas are attractive and magnetic and have a selective quality. When you go public with your idea, you attract people who imagine themselves contributing to your vision. Consider their participation as they seek their own level of interest and compatibility with you as a test run, but realize that their participation may be temporary and limited. Expect this. As an entrepreneur, you're constantly building your dream team in a state of limbo, a composed series of situational relationships. Patching the pieces together in this limbo will eventually create a critical mass, leading to the arrival of unexpected resources and talent. In the end you may find that you have realized your project with the help of people and resources that were entirely unknown to you when you started.

YESTERDAY'S NEWS TOMORROW

While some are seeing the newest thing and copying it religiously, the true innovators are onto something better. Our mass-production society needs style setters, so if your ideas can ride the wave of innovation, you too will be out in front. Draw inspiration from everything, but copy nothing. Imitation will put your creativity on the road to disaster.

STICK AROUND LONG ENOUGH TO BE CREDIBLE

I f you don't meet with success or don't get
in the door the first time, just keep coming
back. When you're trying to gain credibility
with someone, make sure that each interaction
brings something useful. Credibility is not
instantaneous. Eventually, you will be
rewarded for your persistence, as long as
you're sufficiently perceptive. It takes finesse
to be persistent in approaching situations so
that you become someone people want to work
with. If you have a sense that what you're
pursuing is going to be appealing, then you
must persistently advocate your position until
your credibility and the credibility of the idea
are perceived without question.

BENIGN NEGLECT

Leave alone those things that you cannot affect immediately. If nothing can be done about a problem now, minimize the issue and return to it later when the timing is right. Neglect is not a general solution; but when you examine a problem anew, circumstances may have shifted and the need to solve the problem may no longer exist.

THE RESTING PLACE IS
THE LAUNCHING PAD

BOTTOMING OUT BEFORE GOING FORWARD

Thrashing around and getting the lay of the land helps you understand the parameters of success. Along the way you may get hints or inclinations of the right direction to go, but there are always bleak periods when the revelation of how to get to the next step hasn't appeared. Crashing can be good. Be willing to crash in the service of real creativity. If you hit a stone wall, regroup. No matter how talented you are, it's impossible to reach all the right conclusions without help. Out of the chaos of disaster come endless seedlings which grow and take different forms. If you're stuck, you may have to tear your idea apart, put it back out there, and see how it settles. If you don't find what you're seeking right away, and you're resourceful and creative, you're likely to find something even better. Keep your structure movable, flexible, and resilient.

CONNECTIONS ARE THE ESSENCE OF CREATIVITY

Connections are already there. Once you figure out how to connect things in a way others have never seen, you unleash a whole new set of possibilities. The most creative people are those who make the most connections. They understand how a new connection will create its own heat and momentum. If you are in a fertile environment, creativity is easy. People gravitate toward cities and become a part of organizations because complex environments are stimulating and energetic. The problem is when the environment is marginal. It's harder to create when you are isolated and you don't have much input. The real dynamic elements of society are a function of a multitude of connections.

DO IT WELL, FIRST AND ALWAYS

Excellence attracts opportunity. Your idea doesn't have to be big, it just has to be well executed so people can experience and be compelled by it. People want to be a part of excellence. But be wary of insisting on perfection. The constant pursuit of excellence means making each effort as good as possible at the moment of effort. When people say, "Good enough isn't," say, "Good enough *is*." The energy needed to make an idea perfect is often stolen from the energy needed to maintain momentum. Keeping moving is more important than being perfect. You have to understand when to let go and move on. Keep the pot bubbling all the time. Do it as well as you can every time. It doesn't have to be perfect.

CRITICAL MASS OF PERCEPTION

Critical mass—the amount or level of something required for action to occur—is usually thought of as tangible and demonstrable. However, the critical mass of perception is created virtually. It is building a foundation of ideas that makes the perception an accepted reality. Present ideas effectively and convincingly and people will perceive real substance and positive momentum. This perception will cause people to act or change their patterns. Anticipate unspoken objections. Provide visual, technical, and expert support for your ideas. Create models, facsimiles, and other representations that give life to your concept. Expect to present many repetitions of your idea before critical mass is reached.

SYMBOLS SET THE TONE

The character and value of a company are represented by visual symbols. This is reflected in the language and design of a company's website and logo, its advertising and marketing materials, the look of a company's retail or office space, and the caliber of its employees. These symbols set the tone. The public notices when things are out of place even if they are not able to articulate it. Make sure that all of your elements are harmonious. When a business exudes continuity and a consistent vision, a powerful symbolic thesis is created and validated through reinforcement.

BITE THE BULLET AND GET ON WITH THE FUTURE

Projects can turn out badly for many reasons. When things fall apart, consider the costs of continuing to fight for an acceptable result. Remember that time is much more limited than opportunity. When circumstances dictate a change, act with resolve and move on quickly. This may be painful and costly, but recognizing mistakes early will provide the feedback you need to advance elegantly toward future successes.

IDENTIFY YOUR
OPPORTUNITIES IN DISASTER

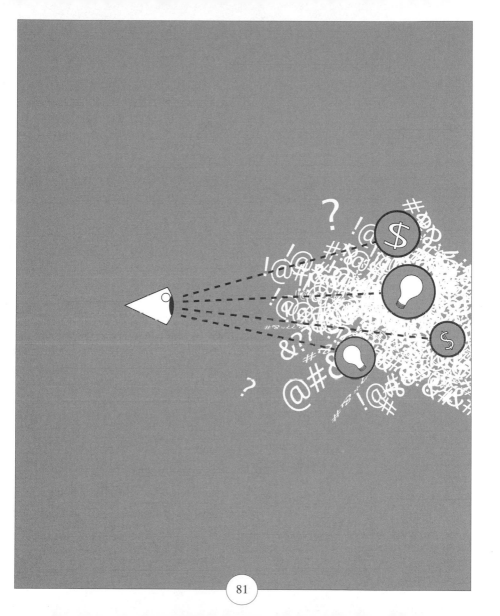

EVERYTHING HAS A PAST
AND DESERVES RESPECT

Honor the past. It is from the past that we borrow the artifacts and ideas needed to create our present moment. Past elements influence us all to differing degrees. What you choose to remember is what you use to move forward. Appreciation of the past is a subtle but powerful influencing factor in what comes next. Remembering the past more deeply gives you more tools to shape the present.

CHAOTIC VIABILITY

Chaotic viability exists when patterns can be recognized in seemingly random and unstructured interactions. Organized hierarchies fail in chaotic environments if their system doesn't allow for novel ideas and solutions. Innovation is necessary to generate productivity from chaos. New solutions are often antithetical to organizational thinking. Entrepreneurs and loose confederations of free thinkers are best suited for working within the fluid vortex of innovation.

THE MORE CREDIBILITY,
THE LESS HARD CASH

Credibility is a form of capital. The more credibility you create, the less hard money you need to realize your idea. Smart people with assets will always need people who can help them. Learn first how to package and position yourself. Credibility is enhanced if you have a track record even if it's in an unrelated field. But if you want to present a very strong package, back it up with some money. Be willing to share the monetary risk.

PARCEL OFF A PIECE
WHEN YOU NEED MONEY

If a business idea is too big to handle and it's draining your resources, get rid of the parts that aren't working. You may lose money in the short term, but you will relieve a burden and increase your general effectiveness. Look at the mass of ideas and strategies you're pursuing, and choose only those pieces that benefit you the most. Eliminate the rest.

LIVE TO FIGHT ANOTHER DAY

YOU CAN'T LET SLEEPING DOGS LIE FOREVER

They say, "Let sleeping dogs lie." Many times, if you are not ready to deal with a problem or situation, you just ignore it. But eventually that dog will wake up, and you should be thinking about what to do when this happens. It's just another way of being prepared for any eventuality even though you don't foresee a problem at the time. Be ready, so when the dog awakes, you'll be able to interact with it.

PAINT IT BIG, KEEP IT SIMPLE

Make your ideas look bigger than they are by doing things that draw attention and generate a big response. Do this by using simple, bold methods. Once you get too intricate, you lose power. Spend your capital on a big sign or something similar that carries maximum impact or speaks with authority. You might have to come back to retool it or redo it, but always present ideas in a way that people recognize as important. Simplicity is best. The easier something is to understand, the more people will respond to it. The public shouldn't have to be specialists to understand your vision. Giving people good quality, good design, and good value is still the best recipe for success.

PROMOTERS
PROMOTING PROMOTERS

The more people promoting a good idea, the more power the idea holds. Promote ideas that open up possibilities and are good for the individual and society. Champion and reward the people who encourage others to perform their tasks well. A promoter promoting promoters operates on a larger scale, promoting the people operating on a smaller scale. When possible, give smaller promoters the benefit of your connections to larger arenas of influence. Create a chain, and greater and broader successes will follow. Support one another and connect promotional capabilities at whatever level possible.

PUTTING PIECES IN PLAY

In chess, each piece, once put into play, has a certain power that affects the strategy and outcome of the game. In business, putting a piece in play might refer to developing a new philosophy or mission statement, adding a new person to the team, or subtracting an element. Adding or eliminating something changes the balance and affects the outcome. Experiment with component parts by reordering them to bring about a new and better result.

KEEP SELLING AFTER
YOU'VE MADE THE DEAL

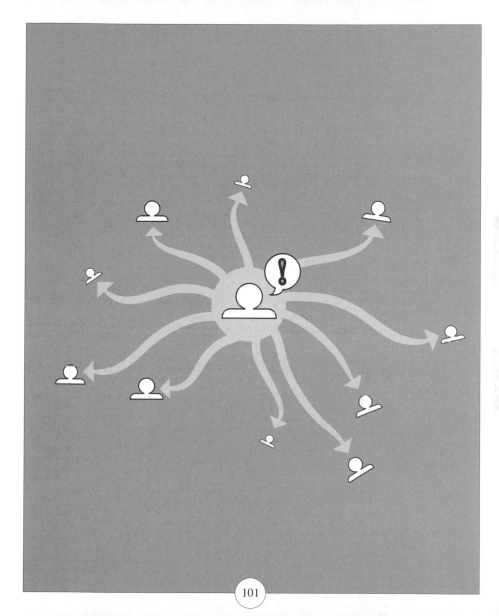

CONVENTIONAL WISDOM IS THE
OPPOSITE OF COMMON SENSE

Conventional wisdom is a synthesis of long-held beliefs—a consensus that people accept as truth. Common sense is looking at all the factors on a here-and-now basis and making a determination as to what is really so. No matter how many rules or patterns have been laid down in the past, they may no longer be relevant. They should be challenged and redirected by those who can look at events in a fresh way. The premise behind much conventional wisdom is often no longer appropriate. If you want to create something different, unusual, and particularly appealing, you need to understand all the characteristics that create new paradigms and develop solutions that are relevant for today.

NEVER QUIT WHEN
YOU ARE RIGHT

Never quit when you know you're right. The idea of what is right evolves, so be aware of intervening factors.Unless something stands in your way that prevents you from seeing clearly, your instincts will lead you to the right result. So persevere because you're on to something.

ABOUT MERRITT

Merritt is Merritt, a unique creative real estate professional and retailer but more retailer than realtor. In 1983, Merritt got to know Mel and Patricia Ziegler, a very creative couple that had started a chain (two small stores and a unique catalog) called Banana Republic Safari & Travel clothing. Merritt thought the Gap should buy the chain. Banana Republic represented about $1M in sales and the Gap was doing about $500M per year. I thought it would be a distraction for us to buy the business, but Merritt persisted and told me how valuable the creativity of the Zieglers would be in growing the business. I agreed and the rest is history. . . Merritt was right.

— Don Fisher, Gap Inc. Founder
and Chairman Emeritus

As someone who, through the years, has signed leases for over 800 stores, I've dealt with all kinds of developers. Merritt Sher, however, is in a class all by himself. He sees things nobody else does, creates unusual projects and picks tenants he knows will succeed. I've never had a bad store with Merritt.

—Warren Eisenberg, Co-Founder and Co-Chairman of Bed Bath & Beyond, Inc.

(Merritt Sher)

photo by Scott Longfield

107

AUTHOR'S BIOGRAPHY

Merritt Sher is widely regarded as one of the country's leading entrepreneurs and real estate innovators. He has created some of America's most successful commercial real estate projects and is credited with developing the first retail "power center" and "lifestyle" center. *Shopping Centers Today* includes Sher in the list of the ten visionaries who have shaped the way Americans shop.

As real estate consultant for The Gap, Merritt arranged the acquisition of Banana Republic. He was a first stage investor and served as chairman of the board of Pacific Sunwear during an early turbulent period. He formed Terranomics, one of the nation's largest retail real estate brokerages, and sold it to Federal Realty Investment Trust in 1995.

In 2001 Sher opened Hotel Healdsburg in California's North Sonoma Wine Country, rated by *Condé Nast Traveler* as one of the top 500 hotels in the world. His advice on entrepreneurial skill building has been featured in *Fortune* magazine and in textbooks. His commitment to ethical development practices informs his revitalization strategies for cities, towns and shopping districts. His counsel is valued by civic leaders nationwide.

Sher graduated from UC Hastings College of the Law. He is married to Pamela Sher, founder of the Hand Fan Museum of Healdsburg, and is the father of three children.